AMAZING DECADES IN PHOTOS

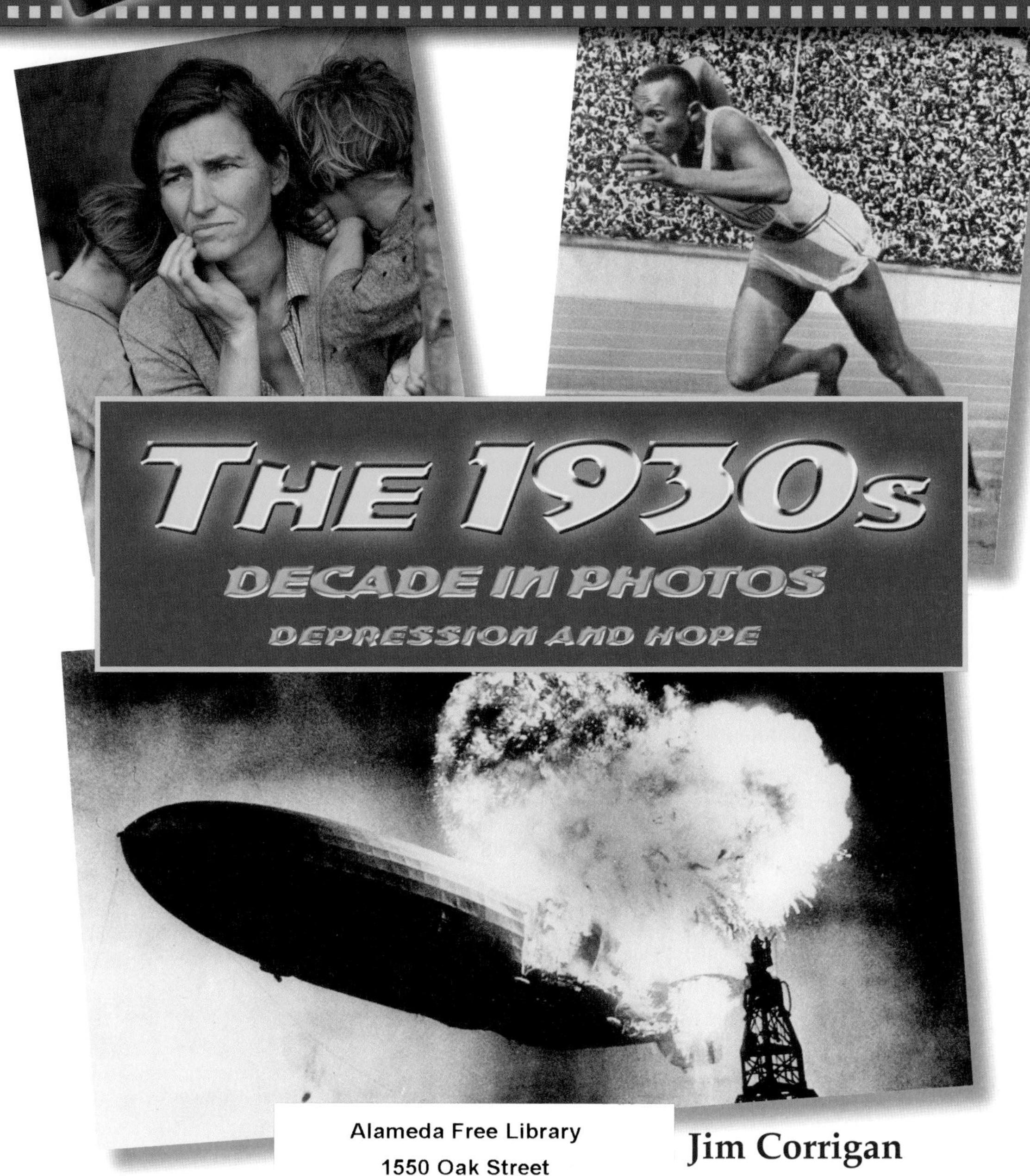

THE 1930s

DECADE IN PHOTOS

DEPRESSION AND HOPE

Jim Corrigan

Enslow Publishers, Inc.
40 Industrial Road
Box 398
Berkeley Heights, NJ 07922
USA
http://www.enslow.com

Library of Congress Cataloging-in-Publication Data

Corrigan, Jim.
The 1930s decade in photos : Depression and hope / by Jim Corrigan.
p. cm. — (Amazing decades in photos)
Includes bibliographical references and index.
Summary: "Middle school readers will find out about the important world, national, and cultural developments of the decade 1930-1939"—Provided by publisher.
ISBN-13: 978-0-7660-3132-6
ISBN-10: 0-7660-3132-2
1. United States—History—1919–1933—Pictorial works—Juvenile literature. 2. United States—History—1933–1945—Pictorial works—Juvenile literature. 3. History, Modern—20th century—Pictorial works—Juvenile literature. 4. Nineteen thirties—Pictorial works—Juvenile literature. I. Title. II. Title: Nineteen thirties decade in photos.
E801.C67 2009
973.917—dc22

2008042904

Printed in the United States of America.

092009 Lake Book Manufacturing, Inc., Melrose Park, IL

10 9 8 7 6 5 4 3 2 1

Produced by OTTN Publishing, Stockton, N.J.

Table of Contents

Unemployed workers register for jobs and file paperwork to receive financial assistance—also known as "relief"—at a state employment office, 1930s. It is estimated that at the height of the Great Depression in 1933, nearly 25 percent of the American work force was unemployed.

Welcome to the 1930s

The 1930s were a troubled time. America and the world were trapped in the Great Depression. Many people had little or no money. They struggled just to find food. Some families lived in cardboard shacks. It was one of the worst economic crises in history. At the time, few people understood how the Great Depression had happened. Nobody knew when it would end.

The previous decade had been a wild and happy time—the Roaring Twenties. People spent money freely. They fell deep into debt. Their actions

Anxious people wait outside the doors of a bank, hoping to withdraw their money before the bank goes out of business, 1933. Thousands of banks failed during the Great Depression.

President Franklin D. Roosevelt created many new government programs intended to help Americans during the Great Depression. One of these was Social Security, also called social insurance. Social Security provides income to Americans who have retired, are unemployed, or can no longer work. Today, over 50 million Americans—about 16 percent of the population—receive Social Security benefits.

were creating unseen problems. The economy was weakening. In 1929, the U.S. stock market crashed. It was the first crisis of the Great Depression. More crises quickly followed. The financial ruin spread across the globe.

Suddenly, stores and factories closed. Millions of workers lost their jobs. Without money, parents could not buy food for their children. They stood in long lines, hoping to get a free loaf of bread or cup of soup. The nation's president, Herbert Hoover, was slow to respond to the disaster. For three years, the government did little to help its suffering citizens.

In 1932, American voters elected a new president: Franklin D. Roosevelt. The fifty-year-old New Yorker was confident. He told Americans that their government had not abandoned them.

As president, Roosevelt did not hesitate. He took decisive action to restart the economy. He created a bold plan called the New Deal. Roosevelt constantly talked to the nation on the radio. He spoke in plain words. His firm voice soothed people's fears. They knew that someone was working hard to help them. Roosevelt always ended his radio talks with a message of encouragement. In short, he gave Americans hope. Americans would reelect Roosevelt four times.

Despite President Roosevelt's efforts, however, the Depression lingered for many years. People grimly went about their lives. They turned to music, movies, and sports to forget about their troubles. They also took pleasure in reading. Newspapers told of heroes such as the daring female pilot Amelia Earhart.

They also reported on outlaws such as Bonnie and Clyde. The kidnapping of a famous baby in 1932 made headlines. So did the fiery crash of a giant airship in 1937. For fiction, readers looked to cheap magazines called pulps. They also enjoyed the adventures of superheroes. Comic books first became popular in the 1930s.

In other countries, the Great Depression was creating political turmoil. In Germany and Japan, dangerous men used the chaos to strengthen their grip on power. These nations became hostile and warlike. As the 1930s drew to a close, the world plunged toward war. World War II began when Germany invaded Poland on September 1, 1939. It would become the deadliest conflict in human history.

Dancers Fred Astaire and Ginger Rogers were two of Hollywood's biggest stars during the 1930s. They starred in many musical films together, including *Top Hat* (1935), *Swing Time* (1936), and *Shall We Dance?* (1937).

Needy farmers in Arizona receive food and other supplies from the government. Beginning in 1933, the U.S. government created relief programs to help people through the Depression.

Descending into Depression

Economists study how money flows through a society in a never-ending cycle. People work at jobs to earn money. With their earnings, they buy goods and services. Companies that sell the goods and services earn a profit. With their profits, companies hire more workers, who buy more goods and services. The cycle continues.

An economy does not always run smoothly. Sometimes the flow of money will slow or even stop. In the 1930s, the U.S. economy broke down. People called the situation the Great Depression. It came as a sudden and great shock. The Roaring Twenties had been a time of economic growth. Jobs were plentiful. Factories turned out a big supply of goods. Some people thought the prosperity would continue forever.

But the U.S. economy had some major problems. Many Americans were plagued by

During the early 1930s, President Herbert Hoover (1874–1964) tried to make things better for businesses.

debt. They bought goods on credit, spending more money than they earned. Eventually, they struggled just to pay back the money they had borrowed. They could not afford new purchases. As a result, the supply of available goods began to exceed the demand for those goods. Factories had to slow down production. America's banks also began struggling. For over a decade, U.S. banks had loaned money without caution. They made risky loans to individuals and foreign governments. Now the banks found that many of their loans were not being paid back. The flow of money was slowing to a trickle. America's economy was grinding to a halt. Yet in spite of these problems, stock prices continued to rise.

Then, in October 1929, the U.S. stock market crashed. People panicked. Many Americans tried to withdraw all their savings from their bank accounts. Banks did not have enough cash to pay everyone. Numerous banks failed, and many Americans lost their life savings. As factories and businesses closed, millions of workers lost their jobs. Large numbers of people also lost their homes. Men wandered the country as hoboes. They jumped on freight trains and went from place to place in search of work and food. In many areas, settlements of crude shacks sprang up on unused land. Homeless people built these shacks from whatever materials they could find: cardboard, bits of wood, pieces of scrap metal. The filthy settlements were called "Hoovervilles," after the president people blamed for doing nothing to stop the economic crisis.

President Herbert Hoover had believed that the economic crisis would not last long. In March 1930, Hoover said that the strain would begin to ease within sixty days. His prediction was wrong. The Great Depression would last more than a decade.

The New York Times.

"All the News That's Fit to Print."

THE WEATHER

STOCKS COLLAPSE IN 16,410,030-SHARE DAY, BUT RALLY AT CLOSE CHEERS BROKERS; BANKERS OPTIMISTIC, TO CONTINUE AID

KAHN REFUSES POST IN SENATE CAMPAIGN; CALLS CHOICE UNWISE

COALITION FIGHTING MOVE TO KILL TARIFF

MISSING AIRLINER BROUGHT IN SAFELY

LEADERS SEE FEAR WANING

Point to 'Lifting Spells' in Trading as Sign of Buying Activity.

CLOSING RALLY VIGOROUS

Leading Issues Regain From 4 to 14 Points in 15 Minutes.

U. S. STEEL TO PAY $1 EXTRA DIVIDEND

RESERVE BOARD FINDS ACTION UNNECESSARY

A *New York Times* headline from October 30, 1929, reports the collapse of the stock market.

The Great Depression affected most industrialized countries during the 1930s. This photo shows British workers marching to protest unemployment and extreme poverty in northeastern England.

The United States was not the only country affected by the Great Depression. In fact, the economic crisis would grip nearly the entire world. Like President Hoover in America, leaders in other countries failed to act effectively when their economies faltered. Trade between nations virtually stopped. Factories everywhere shut down, and many people lost their jobs.

While the Great Depression was felt across the globe, Germany was hit especially hard. The country was still struggling to pay the costs of World War I when the Depression struck. The German economy collapsed. By 1932, almost 40 percent of Germany's workers were unemployed.

Bonus Army Marches on Washington

A person who has served in the military is known as a veteran. In 1924, Congress passed a special law for America's World War I veterans. The law said that each veteran would get a special payment, or bonus, as a reward for fighting in what was then known as the Great War. According to the law, however, the bonuses would not be paid out until 1945.

By the spring of 1932, veterans were tired of waiting for their money. The Great Depression was hard on them, like everyone else. The former soldiers needed money to feed their families. They demanded that their bonuses be paid early. More than seventeen thousand angry veterans from all over the United States went to Washington, D.C., to protest. Newspapers called them the Bonus Army.

In mid-June, the U.S. Senate rejected a bill to pay the bonuses early. Discouraged, some of the veterans who had gone to Washington gave up and went home. But thousands vowed to stay until their demands were met. Some occupied old government buildings not far from the Capitol and the White House. Others lived in camps. The largest of these

Members of the Bonus Army hold a vigil on the lawn outside the U.S. Capitol building, July 13, 1932.

camps was located across the Anacostia River, in an area known as Anacostia Flats.

On July 28, a group of protesters clashed with local police along Pennsylvania Avenue. President Hoover ordered the surrounding area to be cleared of demonstrators. U.S. Army troops under the command of General Douglas MacArthur moved in. MacArthur would become a hero during World War II. But on this day, his conduct was questionable. After forcibly clearing the area around Pennsylvania Avenue, he ignored orders to halt. Instead, MacArthur had his soldiers pursue the retreating veterans across the Anacostia River. A riot broke out. MacArthur's troops destroyed the Bonus Army's camp. They beat Bonus Army veterans. Dozens of the veterans were injured, and at least two died. The incident shocked many Americans. They felt that the violence was unnecessary. Four years later, Congress gave the veterans their early bonus payments.

The Washington Monument looms in the background of this photo of World War I veterans marching to the Capitol in July 1932.

General Douglas MacArthur (left) directs federal troops to evict members of the Bonus Army from their camps. MacArthur (1880–1964) was the highest-ranking officer in the U.S. Army during the early 1930s. He later distinguished himself as a commander in the Pacific during World War II. However, MacArthur's forceful eviction of the Bonus Army is considered one of the most controversial actions of his career.

The Kidnapping of the Century

Charles Augustus Lindbergh Jr. on his first birthday. A few months after this photo was taken, the toddler was kidnapped from his home.

Pilot Charles Lindbergh first became a hero in 1927. That year, he was the first person to fly solo across the Atlantic Ocean. People all over the world celebrated the feat.

Lindbergh remained famous for years. For privacy, he and his wife moved to a quiet estate in New Jersey. They had a baby boy. On March 1, 1932, the small child was kidnapped. The Lindberghs found a ransom note in his nursery. A crude wooden ladder lay beneath the nursery window. The kidnapping would make newspaper headlines for months.

Charles Lindbergh made two ransom payments. However, he never again saw his young son alive. In May 1932, the baby's body was found in a wooded area near the Lindbergh home.

In 1934, a German immigrant named Bruno Hauptmann was arrested for the crime. Hauptmann insisted he was innocent. But at his trial the following year, a jury found him guilty. He was executed in 1936.

Bruno Richard Hauptmann was arrested when he was caught with some of the Lindberghs' ransom money. Other evidence linking Hauptmann to the crime was found at his home. After a six-week trial in early 1935, Hauptmann was convicted of kidnapping and murder.

Press photographers take shots of famous aviator Charles A. Lindbergh (center, without hat) as he leaves the courthouse in Flemington, New Jersey, January 1935. The trial of Bruno Hauptmann attracted international media attention. It has been referred to as the "Trial of the Century."

As a result of the Lindbergh case, Congress changed the nation's kidnapping laws. The new laws gave the FBI more power to investigate kidnappings.

FDR Promises a New Deal

By the fall of 1932, the Great Depression was already three years old. The nation's president, Herbert Hoover, was not very popular. Americans felt that he was insensitive to their suffering.

Franklin D. Roosevelt (1882–1945) shakes hands from the rear platform of a train during his 1932 presidential campaign.

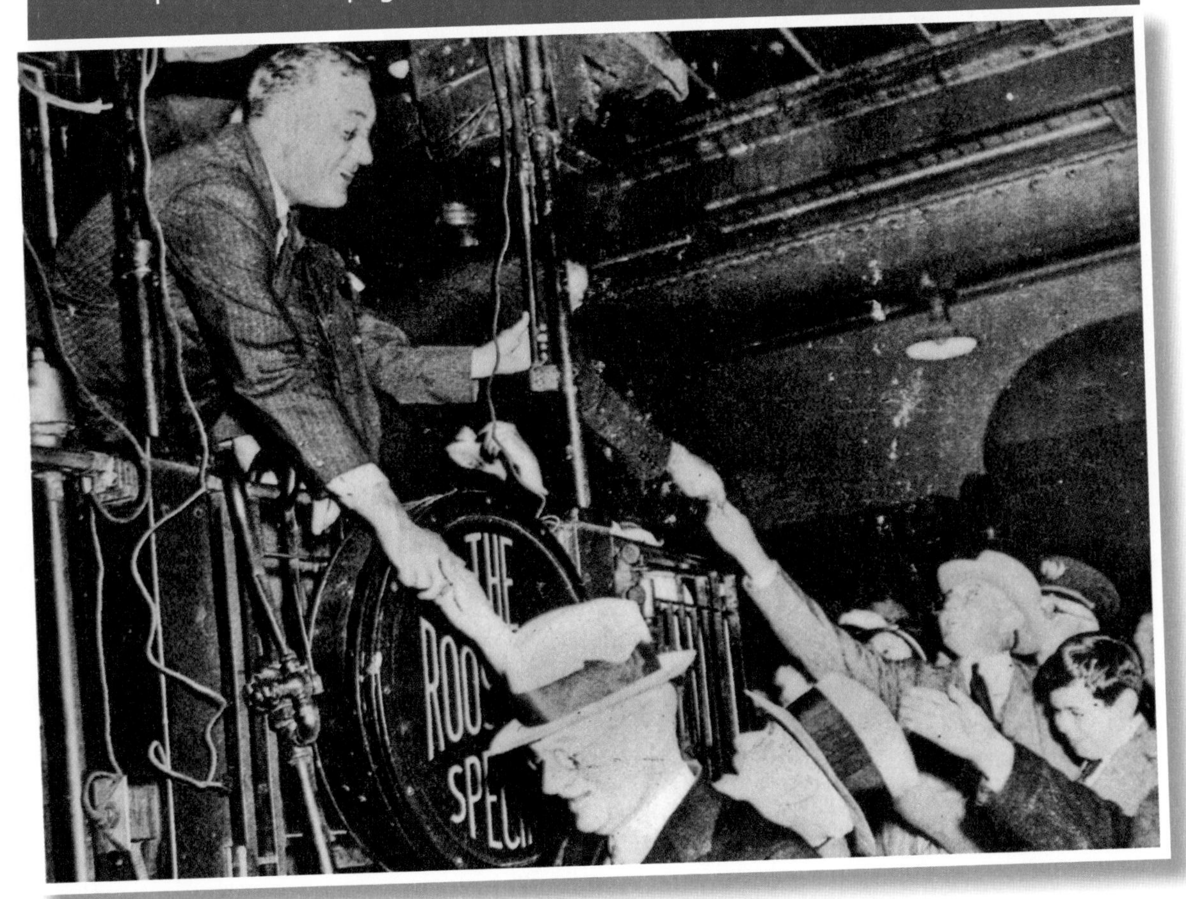

A button from Franklin Roosevelt's first presidential campaign. When he accepted the Democratic Party's nomination for president, Roosevelt made a famous speech. "I pledge you, I pledge myself, to a new deal for the American people," he said.

Still, the Republican Party nominated Hoover for another term as president. His opponent was Democrat Franklin Delano Roosevelt. Since 1929, Roosevelt had been the governor of New York. He was an excellent public speaker. People admired his confidence and concern. Roosevelt campaigned hard for the presidency. He promised a "New Deal" for America. He said that he would do everything possible to end the Depression.

In November, voters went to the polls yearning for change. They wanted a president with spirit and energy. They wanted a leader who would inspire them. Most of all, they wanted someone who would fight the Depression. The voters decided to give Franklin D. Roosevelt a chance. Roosevelt won the election by a wide margin. He was sworn in as president on March 4, 1933.

Roosevelt casts a vote at a New York polling station, November 9, 1932. With him are his wife, Eleanor, and their son, Elliot. Eleanor Roosevelt (1884–1962) was a respected writer and activist who often spoke about the need for equal rights for women and African Americans.

A Hundred Days of Hope

In March 1933, when Franklin D. Roosevelt took office as America's new president, the Great Depression was at its worst. Many banks had closed because of a lack of money. More than 16 million people were out of work. Starving families relied on charity for food.

FDR's first task was to comfort a shaken public. In his first speech as president, he told Americans that "the only thing we have to fear is fear itself." He insisted that the country could beat the Depression if everyone cooperated and worked hard.

Roosevelt got to work right away. He called Congress into an emergency session one day after taking the oath of office. He wanted to enact the first laws of his New Deal program. The laws sought to fix America's broken economy. Congress and the president worked closely together. They wanted to give food to the needy, create jobs for workers, and aid the banks.

Beginning in March 1933, President Roosevelt made informal radio speeches to the American people. He spoke about the country's problems, and the ways in which the government would try to solve them. These speeches became known as "fireside chats."

Roosevelt's "fireside chats" were very popular, attracting millions of listeners. In fact, the chats often drew larger audiences than the most popular radio programs of the 1930s.

During his first hundred days in office, Roosevelt signed into law fifteen major pieces of legislation. These included banking reform laws, emergency relief measures, and jobs programs. The nation was buoyed by the president's vigor, confidence, and dedication. Still, economic recovery would be slow in coming.

President Roosevelt signs the Farm Relief Act, which helped struggling farmers who were having trouble paying their debts, May 12, 1933.

Swinging with the Big Bands

Swing music is a form of jazz. African-American musicians invented jazz. They merged many styles of music into one unique sound. Since its birth in the early 1900s, jazz has continued to evolve. In the 1930s, the evolution of jazz led to swing.

Swing music has a faster beat than other forms of jazz. It is also more formal. Early jazz groups were small. Three or four musicians could easily make changes to songs as they played. Swing bands had twelve to nineteen

The Glenn Miller Orchestra had many hits during the late 1930s and early 1940s. Miller (1904–1944) is standing in front of the band, playing the trombone.

Some of the jazz greats of the 1930s included pianist William "Count" Basie (1904–1984), clarinet player Benny Goodman (1909–1986), and singer Ethel Waters (1896–1977). Goodman developed the swing jazz sound in 1935, and became known as the "King of Swing." Basie also led an important big band during the swing era. Waters was a popular performer at the Cotton Club, a famous nightclub in New York City.

musicians. The large number of performers made it hard to improvise. Instead, the big bands played from carefully arranged sheet music. Drums and bass provided a pulsing rhythm. Saxophones, trumpets, and trombones added lively melody.

Leaders of the best swing bands became famous. In the 1930s, these included Duke Ellington, Count Basie, Benny Goodman, and Glenn Miller. Swing music inspired a number of fast-paced dance steps. The Lindy Hop was named after pilot Charles Lindbergh. Chicago, New York, and Kansas City were swing hot spots. Radio stations carried live big-band performances from these cities.

Many people enjoyed such dance crazes as the jitterbug. This couple dances at a small club in Mississippi in 1939.

This poster shows two young men in Nazi Party uniforms. The poster says that the National Socialists are making sacrifices to create a new Germany, and asks voters to choose the party in the 1932 election.

The Nazis Take Control of Germany

Germany lost World War I in 1918. It never fully recovered from the defeat. For a decade after the war, the German economy struggled. Then the Great Depression came. It struck the nation hard. German citizens desperately wanted change. They looked toward the radical Nazi Party and Adolf Hitler. (Nazi is short for Nationalsozialistische Deutsche Arbeiterpartei, or the National Socialist German Workers' Party.)

By 1932, Hitler and the Nazis were well known in Germany. They had tried to overthrow the government in 1923. The following year, Hitler went on trial for treason. While serving a nine-month prison term, Hitler wrote *Mein Kampf* (or *My Struggle*). The book described his political beliefs. It was a best seller.

The Nazis became popular by blaming others for Germany's troubles. They blamed the German government for losing World War I. The peace treaty forced Germany to give up land, money, and natural resources. Germany's mighty army

Adolf Hitler (1889–1945) gives the Nazi Party salute as soldiers wearing the party uniform march past his car, 1935.

was reduced to a small force. Hitler told the German people that their leaders had betrayed them. Many people believed his words.

The Great Depression made life even harder for the German people. But it helped the Nazi Party. Germany's democratic government grew weaker. Meanwhile, Nazis began winning seats in Germany's parliament, or legislature. In the elections of 1932, the Nazi Party scored many victories. Adolf Hitler was appointed the nation's chancellor. Hitler promptly turned Germany into a police state. All traces of freedom and democracy soon vanished.

The Nazis controlled the lives of all German citizens, including children. Schools taught Nazi ideas. Boys were required to join the Hitler Youth. Girls were forced to join the League of German Girls. These clubs surrounded children with Nazi culture.

An enormous crowd of Germans waits for Hitler to appear at a public rally, 1937.

When the Nazis came to power, they cracked down on Jews living in Germany. Eventually, the German authorities began arresting Jewish families and sending them to concentration camps, where they were murdered or forced to work as slaves. This contemporary photo shows the main entrance at Auschwitz, one of the most infamous concentration camps.

Adults were constantly exposed to Nazi culture, too. Hitler ensured that all newspapers, books, and radio shows praised Nazi ideals. Propaganda seeped into every facet of German life. The Nazis held enormous rallies. Hundreds of thousands of people attended them. The rallies created a sense of unity. People became completely devoted to Adolf Hitler.

The democratic government was gone. The Nazis could no longer blame it for the country's problems. They needed a new target to blame. They focused on Germany's minority peoples. Even before they came to power, the Nazis had spewed hateful words at people of Jewish descent. Now Jews felt the full brunt of that hatred. The Nazis built prisons called concentration camps. At these horrible places, Jews and other unwanted people faced slave labor, torture, and death.

Hitler ignored Germany's commitment to keep its army small. In the coming years, he would create an immense war machine. Germany became a threat to its European neighbors. Throughout the 1930s, Adolf Hitler planned his conquests.

Prohibition Is Repealed

America's thirteen-year ban on alcohol had failed. Prohibition was meant to reduce crime. Instead, it made gangsters powerful. They grew rich selling alcohol illegally. President Roosevelt wanted to make liquor legal again. Most of the public supported him.

During the 1932 election, the Democratic Party promised to repeal the Eighteenth Amendment, which had made it illegal to manufacture, sell, or transport alcoholic beverages. "Happy Days are Here Again" was the title of a popular song from the era. It was used as Franklin D. Roosevelt's campaign anthem.

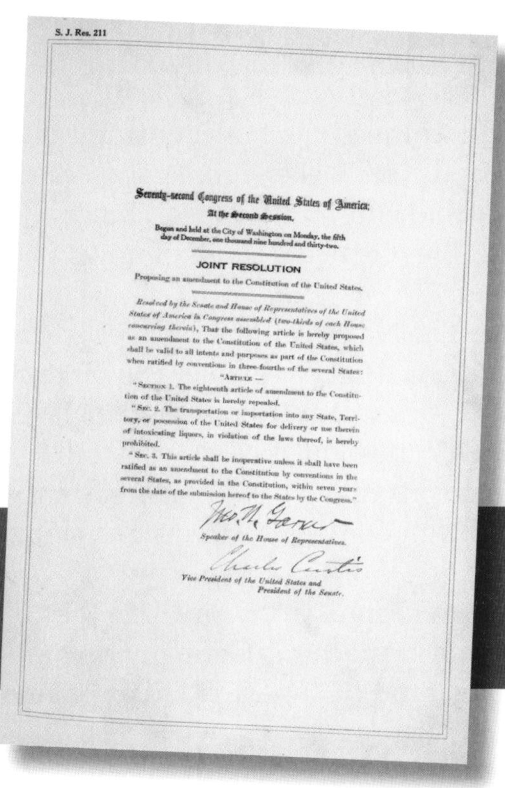

S. J. Res. 211

Seventy-second Congress of the United States of America;
At the Second Session,

Begun and held at the City of Washington on Monday, the fifth day of December, one thousand nine hundred and thirty-two.

JOINT RESOLUTION

Proposing an amendment to the Constitution of the United States.

Resolved by the Senate and House of Representatives of the United States of America in Congress assembled (two-thirds of each House concurring therein), That the following article is hereby proposed as an amendment to the Constitution of the United States, which shall be valid to all intents and purposes as part of the Constitution when ratified by conventions in three-fourths of the several States:

"Article —

"Section 1. The eighteenth article of amendment to the Constitution of the United States is hereby repealed.

"Sec. 2. The transportation or importation into any State, Territory, or possession of the United States for delivery or use therein of intoxicating liquors, in violation of the laws thereof, is hereby prohibited.

"Sec. 3. This article shall be inoperative unless it shall have been ratified as an amendment to the Constitution by conventions in the several States, as provided in the Constitution, within seven years from the date of the submission hereof to the States by the Congress."

Speaker of the House of Representatives.

Vice President of the United States and President of the Senate.

The Twenty-first Amendment, which ended Prohibition, was ratified on December 5, 1933, when Utah became thirty-sixth of the forty-eight states to approve the measure.

Workers hold up cases of beer on top of a delivery truck. They are celebrating the end of Prohibition.

Prohibition first began in 1920. At the time, many people felt that outlawing alcohol would make America a better place. They thought that society would be more wholesome and productive. It was a noble idea, but it did not work. Drinkers did not simply forget about alcohol. Instead, they found illegal ways of obtaining it. Smugglers brought liquor from other countries. It was served in secret nightclubs. Alcohol became more tempting.

The Twenty-first Amendment to the Constitution was ratified in 1933. It said that alcohol was no longer illegal. Gangsters could no longer profit from its sale. The government began taxing legal liquor sales. These taxes helped the government fight the Great Depression.

The Legend of Bonnie and Clyde

Bonnie Parker and Clyde Barrow posed for this photo during their 1932–1934 crime spree. Although Bonnie and Clyde were murderous criminals, some people admired them. People who had lost their life savings because of bank failures were angry at bankers. Some saw the adventures of Bonnie and Clyde as a modern-day version of the Robin Hood story, in which the robbers were striking a symbolic blow against the wealthy.

Bonnie Parker and Clyde Barrow were criminals. They robbed gas stations, stores, and banks. Bonnie and Clyde were both from Texas and were in their early twenties. They led a gang that included six other people. Among these people were Clyde's brother, Marvin Barrow, and Marvin's wife, Blanche. From 1932 to 1934, the Barrow Gang ran wild through the south-central United States.

Clyde Barrow had been in trouble with the law since his teens. Before joining him, Bonnie Parker was a waitress. She enjoyed writing poetry and smoking cigars. The Barrow Gang usually eluded police. Sometimes they escaped only after a fierce gun battle.

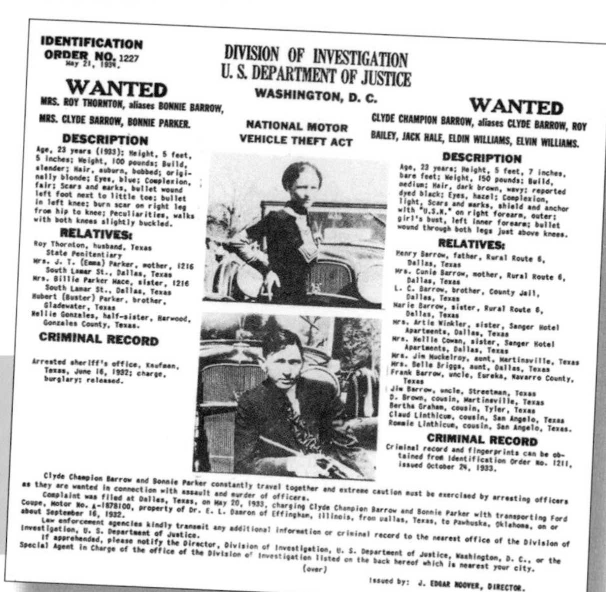

IDENTIFICATION ORDER NO. 1227
May 21, 1934.

DIVISION OF INVESTIGATION
U. S. DEPARTMENT OF JUSTICE
WASHINGTON, D. C.

NATIONAL MOTOR VEHICLE THEFT ACT

WANTED

MRS. ROY THORNTON, aliases BONNIE BARROW, MRS. CLYDE BARROW, BONNIE PARKER.

DESCRIPTION

Age, 23 years (1933); Height, 5 feet, 5 inches; Weight, 100 pounds; Build, slender; Hair, auburn, bobbed; originally blonde; Eyes, blue; Complexion, fair; Scars and marks, bullet wound left foot next to little toe; bullet in left knee; burn scar on right leg from hip to knee; Peculiarities, walks with both knees slightly buckled.

RELATIVES:

Roy Thornton, husband, Texas State Penitentiary
Mrs. J. T. (Emma) Parker, mother, 1216 South Lamar St., Dallas, Texas
Mrs. Billie Parker Mace, sister, 1216 South Lamar St., Dallas, Texas
Hubert (Buster) Parker, brother, Gladewater, Texas
Nellie Gonzales, half-sister, Harwood, Gonzales County, Texas.

CRIMINAL RECORD

Arrested sheriff's office, Kaufman, Texas, June 16, 1932; charge, burglary; released.

WANTED

CLYDE CHAMPION BARROW, aliases CLYDE BARROW, ROY BAILEY, JACK HALE, ELDIN WILLIAMS, ELVIN WILLIAMS.

DESCRIPTION

Age, 23 years; Height, 5 feet, 7 inches, bare feet; Weight, 150 pounds; Build, medium; Hair, dark brown, wavy; reported dyed black; Eyes, hazel; Complexion, light, Scars and marks, shield and anchor with "U.S.N." on right forearm, outer; girl's bust, left inner forearm; bullet wound through both legs just above knees.

RELATIVES:

Henry Barrow, father, Rural Route 6, Dallas, Texas
Mrs. Cunie Barrow, mother, Rural Route 6, Dallas, Texas
L. C. Barrow, brother, County Jail, Dallas, Texas
Marie Barrow, sister, Rural Route 6, Dallas, Texas
Mrs. Artie Winkler, sister, Sanger Hotel Apartments, Dallas, Texas
Mrs. Nellie Cowan, sister, Sanger Hotel Apartments, Dallas, Texas
Mrs. Jim Muckelroy, aunt, Martinsville, Texas
Mrs. Belle Briggs, aunt, Dallas, Texas
Frank Barrow, uncle, Eureka, Navarro County, Texas
Jim Barrow, uncle, Streetman, Texas
D. Brown, cousin, Martinsville, Texas
Bertha Graham, cousin, Tyler, Texas
Claud Linthicum, cousin, San Angelo, Texas
Rommie Linthicum, cousin, San Angelo, Texas.

CRIMINAL RECORD

Criminal record and fingerprints can be obtained from Identification Order No. 1211, issued October 24, 1933.

Clyde Champion Barrow and Bonnie Parker constantly travel together and extreme caution must be exercised by arresting officers as they are wanted in connection with assault and murder of officers.

Complaint was filed at Dallas, Texas, on May 20, 1933, charging Clyde Champion Barrow and Bonnie Parker with transporting Ford Coupe, Motor No. A-1878100, property of Dr. E. L. Damron of Effingham, Illinois, from Dallas, Texas, to Pawhuska, Oklahoma, on or about September 16, 1932.

Law enforcement agencies kindly transmit any additional information or criminal record to the nearest office of the Division of Investigation, U. S. Department of Justice.

If apprehended, please notify the Director, Division of Investigation, U. S. Department of Justice, Washington, D. C., or the Special Agent in Charge of the office of the Division of Investigation listed on the back hereof which is nearest your city.

(over)

Issued by: J. EDGAR HOOVER, DIRECTOR.

This wanted poster was issued in 1934 by the Division of Investigation (now called the Federal Bureau of Investigation, or FBI). Police officers were warned to approach the duo with "extreme caution."

Americans read about the gang's adventures in newspapers. Some people began cheering for Bonnie and Clyde. They enjoyed reading the tales of the two young lovers. The gang always released its hostages unharmed after an escape. Bonnie and Clyde often gave the freed hostages money to get home. To many people, it all seemed like harmless fun. In reality, Bonnie and Clyde were suspected of committing more than a dozen murders.

Public opinion turned against Bonnie and Clyde in April 1934. The gang killed two Texas policemen in cold blood. A month later, Bonnie and Clyde were caught in a police ambush near Arcadia, Louisiana. They died in a hail of bullets.

Today, the legend of Bonnie and Clyde continues to fascinate people. The story of the young outlaws has been told in numerous books and films.

Several movies have been made about the Barrow Gang. This is a scene from one of the most famous films, *Bonnie and Clyde*. The 1967 film won two Academy Awards.

Devastation of the Dust Bowl

Today, we know that our actions can harm the environment. In the 1930s, that fact was not clearly understood. Farmers in America's Midwest accidentally caused a tragedy. The region became a barren wasteland. Giant dust storms blotted out the sun. Dirt fell from the sky like snow. The environmental disaster was called the Dust Bowl.

The prairies of the Midwest have always been prone to drought. Native grasses protected the land. They kept windstorms from carrying away dry soil.

A dust storm approaches a Texas farmhouse in this photo taken on April 18, 1935. During the 1930s a single dust storm in the Midwest could linger for days.

A migrant farm worker holds an infant outside his home on the edge of a pea field in California's Imperial Valley, 1937. The Dust Bowl forced hundreds of thousands of Americans to leave their farms in the Midwest. These migrants were sometimes called "Okies," because many of them came from Oklahoma. Migrants often traveled to California, where they found work picking fruit or other crops for low wages.

Farmers did not realize the importance of the grass. They removed it to plant their crops. In doing so, they exposed the fine topsoil beneath to harmful wind.

A series of droughts struck the region in the early 1930s. Portions of Kansas, Oklahoma, Texas, New Mexico, and Colorado turned into disaster zones. Powerful windstorms carried away the dry soil. Huge dust clouds swept across the landscape. The sky grew black as far away as the East Coast. Farmers' lives were ruined. Thousands took their families and moved away.

Those who remained learned to farm the land properly. The government helped them find ways to protect the soil. One way was by planting rows of trees around crop fields, which helped break the wind. Slowly, the Midwest once again became fruitful.

A group of boys plays with marbles at a Farm Security Administration camp for migrant workers in Texas. The Farm Security Administration (FSA) was a government agency created in 1935 to help farmers affected by the Dust Bowl. It was part of Roosevelt's New Deal program.

The New Deal Begins to Work

By 1934, America was in the fifth year of the Great Depression. One in six people still relied on charity to stay alive. They desperately wanted to work, but no jobs were available.

Roosevelt had promised Americans a "New Deal." His plan was to create new jobs for people. They would work for the government. President Roosevelt had them build roads, bridges, schools, and libraries. The laborers earned enough money to feed their families. At the same time, the work they did made America a more developed, stronger nation.

Beginning in 1935, the Works Progress Administration (WPA) provided jobs to millions of unemployed Americans. Most WPA projects involved construction of public buildings, parks, bridges, utilities, and roadways. The Works Progress Administration was the largest New Deal agency.

One of the first New Deal programs was creation of the Tennessee Valley Authority (TVA) in March 1933. This government-owned corporation was created to bring electricity to the Tennessee Valley, a region in the southern United States. People living in this area were among the poorest Americans. The TVA built many dams, such as the one being constructed here, to generate electricity.

FDR's New Deal programs offered a job for nearly every type of worker. Musicians were hired to perform concerts. Teachers taught illiterate adults how to read. Authors were paid to write children's books. Strong young men built national parks, planted trees, and fought forest fires.

Most New Deal programs disappeared once the Depression ended. A few still exist today. One important reform that still exists is Social Security. Through Social Security, workers pay taxes to aid disabled people who cannot work, and to make sure the workers themselves have money when they retire. The program helps keep people out of poverty.

Members of the Civilian Conservation Corps (CCC) plant small trees on a hillside to prevent soil erosion—a major problem in the Dust Bowl region. The CCC employed many young men in projects related to natural conservation. These included caring for forests on public lands, constructing fences, and building logging and fire roads in rural areas.

The National Recovery Administration (NRA) was an attempt to stabilize prices and establish a minimum wage for workers during the Great Depression. Businesses that participated in the program could display a poster with the NRA's symbol, a blue eagle. Although workers liked the program, the Supreme Court ruled in 1935 that the NRA was unconstitutional.

Fiery Crash of the *Hindenburg*

Airships are huge, cigar-shaped aircraft that are kept aloft by a lighter-than-air gas. During the 1930s, airships were an elegant way to travel. Some carried passengers across the Atlantic Ocean. In 1937, however, there was a terrible airship accident.

This photo was taken at almost the split second that the *Hindenburg* exploded above the Lakehurst Naval Air Station in May 1937.

A German poster from 1936 shows an airship flying across the Atlantic Ocean. Airships like the *Hindenburg* could fly up to 85 miles per hour. This enabled them to cross the Atlantic in about three days—faster than a ship.

The *Hindenburg* was a German airship. It was 804 feet long. That is longer than three jumbo jets placed end-to-end. Like other airships, the *Hindenburg* was made of a steel frame covered by a fabric "skin." Inside the massive airship was a dining room, a lounge, a smoking room, and private cabins. The *Hindenburg* could carry up to seventy passengers plus the crew. Hydrogen gas, which was contained in cells, kept it aloft. A trip on the *Hindenburg* was very expensive. Only wealthy people could afford to fly on the ship.

On May 6, 1937, the *Hindenburg* was approaching Lakehurst, New Jersey. It had just crossed the Atlantic. People gathered on the ground to watch it land. Everything seemed normal. Suddenly, the *Hindenburg* burst into flames. It crashed to the ground. The fire burned rapidly, fueled by the *Hindenburg*'s fabric skin and by the hydrogen. The destruction of the *Hindenburg* took less than a minute.

Remarkably, nearly two-thirds of the people aboard survived. Thirty-five passengers and crew members died. So did one person on the ground. The cause of the accident has never been determined.

Hindenburg crashes to earth, tail first, in flaming ruins. The deadly disaster ended regular passenger service by airships.

During the 1930s, this palace in Geneva, Switzerland, served as the headquarters for the League of Nations. The League was formed after the end of the First World War. It was meant to provide a way for countries to settle their problems through negotiation, rather than resorting to warfare.

The League of Nations Falters

The League of Nations was created after World War I. It was a group of forty-two countries. They hoped to work together to avoid future wars. The League of Nations struggled during the 1930s. Powerful dictators were threatening war. In the end, the League was helpless to stop them.

Diplomats take a break during the first session of the League of Nations in November 1920.

Ethiopian leader Haile Selassie asks the League of Nations for help during Italy's 1935–1936 invasion of his country. When the League tried to intervene, Italy simply withdrew from the organization and completed its conquest of the African nation.

The League of Nations had first been proposed by an American president, Woodrow Wilson. But the United States never joined. This weakened the League. There were other problems as well. Member countries continued to act selfishly. They would not compromise for the benefit of all. Even worse, the League was unable to punish hostile nations. In 1931, the Japanese army invaded Manchuria, in northeastern China. Japan soon conquered the region. In 1933, the League of Nations ordered Japan to pull out of Manchuria. Japan refused, and its diplomats walked out of the League meeting.

Other nations quickly noticed the League's weakness. Adolf Hitler canceled Germany's membership shortly after he came to power. In 1935, Italian dictator Benito Mussolini invaded the African nation of Ethiopia. Mussolini ignored the League's criticism. For the rest of the decade, Japan, Germany, and Italy would continue their aggressive policies. The League was unable to deter them. The world slowly drifted closer to another war.

Legacy of the League

Despite its many flaws, the League of Nations was valuable. It was an important first step toward global cooperation. Eventually, the United Nations would replace it. The United Nations learned from the League's mistakes. Today, diplomats from 192 countries meet at the U.N. headquarters in New York City.

A view of national flags flying outside the United Nations building in New York. The United Nations was created to replace the League of Nations at the end of World War II.

Sports in the Spotlight

Athletics are good exercise and entertainment. However, in the 1930s sports took on more importance. Some events grew beyond a contest between athletes. They became part of a rivalry between nations and races.

Jesse Owens was an African-American track star. In 1936, he went to Berlin, Germany. Adolf Hitler's Nazi Germany was hosting the Summer Olympics. The Nazis believed that certain groups of people—such as Jews and blacks—were inferior. Jesse Owens stunned his hosts with a superb performance. Owens captured four gold medals in the sprint and long jump events.

Jesse Owens (1913–1980) bursts from the starting line in the 200-meter dash at the 1936 Olympic Games. Owens became an international hero by winning gold medals in the 100 meters, 200 meters, long jump, and as a member of an American relay team.

Max Schmeling tries to rise from the canvas after being knocked down by Joe Louis, June 22, 1938. The African-American Louis (1914–1981) is considered one of the greatest heavyweight boxers of all time.

Germans and African-Americans also clashed in professional boxing. A huge match took place in New York in 1936. German heavyweight Max Schmeling fought African-American boxer Joe Louis. The powerful Louis suffered his first loss. Max Schmeling returned to Germany a hero. The rivalry was not over, however. In a 1938 rematch, Joe Louis easily defeated Schmeling in just one round.

"Match of the Century"

Horse racing was hugely popular in the 1930s. One race in 1938 was dubbed the "Match of the Century." It pitted a small, spirited horse named Seabiscuit against the powerful champion War Admiral. The match took place at Pimlico in Maryland on November 1. Many Americans were rooting for the underdog Seabiscuit. They cheered him on to a stunning upset victory.

Seabiscuit leads War Admiral in their 1938 match race. Unlike a regular horse race, which usually includes six to twelve horses, a match race includes only two contenders. A crowd of about forty thousand people came to see the race at Pimlico Race Course in Maryland. Forty million more listened to Seabiscuit's victory over the radio.

Amelia Earhart Disappears

Amelia Earhart was a famous pilot. She enjoyed setting records. In 1928, Earhart became the first woman to fly an airplane across the Atlantic Ocean. Four years later, she set a new speed record for the crossing. Earhart wrote books about her many adventures. She also helped design airplanes.

In 1937, Earhart tried to fly around the world. Other pilots had circled the globe before her. However, Earhart planned to follow the longest possible route. She would fly close to the equator. The first attempt failed when her plane broke down in Hawaii. For her second try, Earhart decided to fly in the opposite direction. She and navigator Fred Noonan left from Miami, Florida. They headed out over the Atlantic.

In 1932, Amelia Earhart (1897-1937?) became the first woman to receive the Distinguished Flying Cross. She had served as navigator during her first flight across the Atlantic Ocean, in 1928. In 1932, she became the first woman to pilot an airplane across the Atlantic.

This Lockheed Vega, flown by Amelia Earhart across the Atlantic Ocean in 1932, is on display at the National Air and Space Museum in Washington, D.C.

After four weeks, Earhart and Noonan had completed three-quarters of their journey. They had flown an incredible 22,000 miles. On July 2, 1937, they neared Howland Island in the central Pacific. But their twin-engine plane never reached the island. It simply disappeared. The U.S. Navy and Coast Guard searched frantically for Amelia Earhart and Fred Noonan. No trace of them or their aircraft was ever found.

Amelia Earhart and her navigator, Fred Noonan, pose in front of their twin-engine Lockheed Electra in Los Angeles, 1937. Some people believe that their plane ran out of fuel and crashed into the ocean. Others believe that the plane crashed on an uninhabited island in the western Pacific Ocean. But although people continue to search for clues, no one really knows what happened to Amelia Earhart.

From Pulp Fiction to Comic Books

During the Great Depression, many people could not afford books. But they could still enjoy reading by turning to cheap magazines. For a dime or less, readers could escape into a world of adventure and superheroes.

Low-cost magazines were printed on cheap, grainy paper called pulp. They had titles like *Amazing Stories*, *Dime Detective*, and *Flying Aces*. Pulp magazines contained short stories of action and adventure. Often these stories were poorly written. Publishers relied on colorful and exciting cover art to sell their magazines. Artists created dazzling images of horror, mystery, science fiction, and romance. Authors then wrote stories that matched the cover art. Despite their low quality, pulp magazines were fun and amusing.

Comic books also became standard reading in the 1930s. They began as reprints of newspaper cartoons. Readers were won over. Soon, brand-new comics appeared on newsstands. Comic book sales soared in 1938. That year, Superman made his debut in *Action Comics*. A year later, Batman made his first appearance in *Detective Comics*. The superheroes quickly gained legions of young readers.

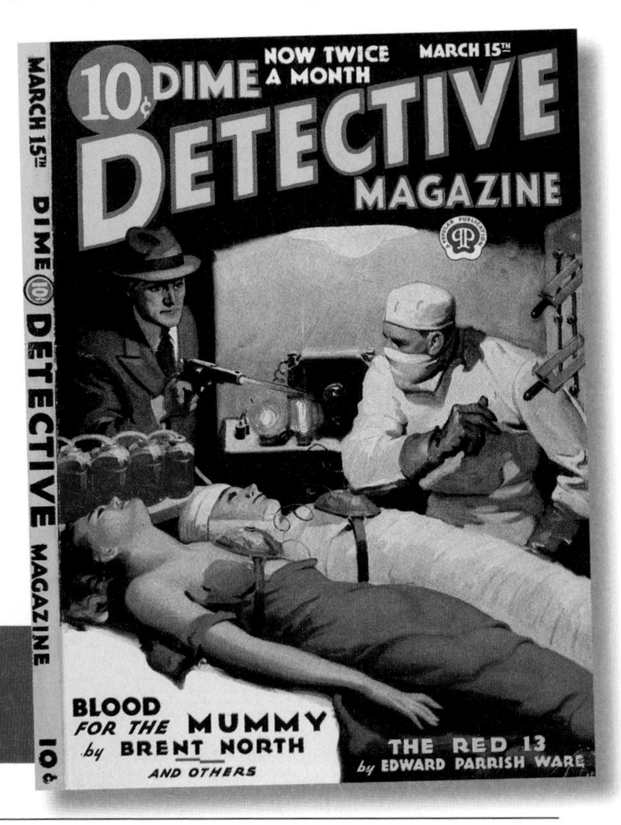

Pulp magazines, sometimes called "dime novels," often featured exciting or shocking covers to attract readers.

Writer Jerry Siegel and artist Joe Shuster created the comic book character of Superman during the 1930s. They envisioned him as a hero who would fight for the downtrodden. Superman's exploits appealed to Americans struggling through the Great Depression.

Golden Age of Hollywood

Early films had no color or sound. They were black-and-white and silent. By the 1930s, the technology for color and sound had arrived. Studios began making bright, beautiful films. Huge crowds anxiously packed into movie theaters. It was the golden age of Hollywood.

Gone with the Wind won ten Academy Awards, including the Oscar for Best Picture. The movie is set in the South during and after the American Civil War.

Charlie Chaplin's 1936 silent comedy *Modern Times* examined the problems of industrialization. It is considered one of Chaplin's finest films.

Walt Disney was a skilled animator. From his tiny studio, he created charming cartoon characters. Disney dreamed of making a full-length animated film. It was a difficult challenge. Cartoons were usually just a few minutes long. They were expensive and time-consuming to make. An animated film would require much money and an army of artists. Disney did not give up. His reward came in 1937 with the release of *Snow White and the Seven Dwarfs*. The film became a classic.

Another classic movie debuted two years later, in 1939. *Gone with the Wind* was based on the award-winning novel by Margaret Mitchell. It was about life in the South during and after the Civil War. *Gone with the Wind* sold more tickets than any other film in Hollywood history. The record still stands today.

When *The Wizard of Oz* was released in 1939, it was a popular film. However, it was overshadowed by the success of *Gone with the Wind*. Today, both *The Wizard of Oz* and *Gone with the Wind* are ranked among the greatest movies of all time.

Japanese soldiers cheer as they hoist their flag from the roof of a central government building in Nanjing, the capital of China. (Today, the capital is Beijing.) After the capture of Nanjing on December 13, 1937, Japanese troops murdered thousands of Chinese civilians. The Japanese also looted businesses, tortured people, and burned down homes and buildings.

Japan Launches All-Out War Against China

Japan is a nation of islands. The islands have few natural resources. China is Japan's neighbor. China is huge and has vast natural resources. In the 1930s, Japan's army was growing rapidly. Japanese leaders wanted China's land and resources. The Japanese army slowly seized pieces of Chinese territory. By 1937, the two nations were locked in a full-scale war.

The events leading to war had begun years earlier. Since the 1920s, Japan was completely under the control of its military. Japanese citizens worked solely toward building the armed forces. They created a powerful war machine. The officers in charge, meanwhile, made plans. They wanted to expand the Japanese Empire. China was an obvious place to start. It was nearby and poorly defended. China also had large

General Chiang Kai-shek (1887–1975) examines a map with other Chinese officers during a military campaign, 1930s. Chiang (right) led the resistance when Japan invaded China in 1937.

amounts of iron, coal, and open land. Japan desperately wanted those raw materials and that land.

The situation in China was very different. In 1911, that nation underwent a revolution. The revolution ended more than two thousand years of rule by emperors. Afterward, rival groups fought for control of the country. The two major groups were the Nationalists, led by Chiang Kai-shek, and the Communists, led by Mao Zedong. Their ongoing fight weakened China and put it at risk of invasion by a foreign country.

Japan's army began its conquest in 1931. For the next six years, the Japanese made small but steady gains. During this time, China's warring groups fought with each other as much as they did with the invaders.

In July 1937, heavy fighting broke out. Japanese troops moved on Beijing. The Nationalists and the Communists finally agreed to set aside their differences. They united against a common enemy. Japan and China were officially at war. The early months of the war went poorly for the Chinese.

Burned and abandoned, this terrified Chinese baby cries in the ruins of a train station in Shanghai that was destroyed in a Japanese air raid. Japanese attacks during the war killed millions of civilians.

A company of Japanese soldiers cheers while standing on a section of the Great Wall of China.

They were constantly forced to retreat. The Japanese soldiers had better weapons and training.

Within six months, Japan's army reached the walled city of Nanjing. At the time, Nanjing was China's capital. Once inside, Japanese soldiers ravaged the city. For six weeks, they tortured and murdered its residents. The death toll from the Nanjing massacre is unknown. However, modern estimates place it between 150,000 and 300,000 people.

The brutal war would drag on for years. Chinese forces continued to retreat. The Japanese soldiers followed them deeper into Chinese territory. Japan's war in China would eventually sap its military strength. It would also hamper Japan's efforts against America in World War II.

Polish children stand in a rubble-filled street in Warsaw, September 1939. The German invasion of Poland marked the beginning of World War II.

WORLD WAR II BEGINS

World War II was the largest conflict in human history. It began in 1939. In the years before the war, Germany became increasingly aggressive. Dictator Adolf Hitler planned to conquer Europe. To achieve his goal, Hitler built an enormous army, navy, and air force.

Britain and France watched the events in Germany with concern. When World War I ended, Germany had pledged to keep its military forces small. Adolf Hitler ignored that promise. He knew that other nations hoped to avoid

German troops march into Austria, March 1938. The *Anschluss,* or unification of Germany and the neighboring country of Austria, was the first step in Hitler's plan to gain control of Europe. Many German-speaking Austrians welcomed the Germans.

another war. The horror of World War I was still a bitter memory. Hitler felt he could break Germany's pledge and nobody would stop him. He proceeded with his plans. Soon Germany brimmed with well-trained troops and powerful weapons.

By 1938, Hitler was ready to begin his conquest. First, he sent German troops into Austria. Next, he looked to the western region of Czechoslovakia. It was known as the Sudetenland. Hitler threatened to take the Sudetenland by force. Leaders in Britain and France grew alarmed. They called a meeting to discuss the matter. Diplomats gathered in the German city of Munich. At Munich, Britain and France agreed to give Germany the Sudetenland. In return, Hitler promised not to take any more territory. At the time, many people believed the Munich Pact would guarantee peace. In reality, it only made Hitler bolder and more warlike. The German leader was convinced Britain and France would not stand in his way.

British Prime Minister Neville Chamberlain holds up a copy of the Munich Pact. In negotiations with Germany during September 1938, Chamberlain offered to give Hitler the Sudetenland territory. In exchange, he asked Hitler to promise not to attack any other countries. This negotiating tactic is called appeasement. However, it did not work. Although Chamberlain assured the British people that the Munich Pact would mean "peace for our time," Germany soon continued its aggression.

By October 1939, German soldiers like the ones pictured above had conquered most of Poland. The German army then prepared to attack the countries of Western Europe.

Six months later, Adolf Hitler brazenly broke his Munich promise. He invaded the rest of Czechoslovakia. The British and French realized they had been fooled. Their attempt to satisfy Hitler by giving him the Sudetenland had failed. His next target appeared to be the nation of Poland. Britain and France warned him that any attack on Poland would be grounds for war.

Hitler ignored these warnings. He felt confident that Britain and France were just making empty threats. He was more concerned about the Soviet Union. A war with that huge nation was not yet in Hitler's plans. In August 1939, he signed a treaty with the Soviet Union. It said that Germany and the Soviet Union would not attack one another in the event of a European war. Hitler would eventually break that pact as well.

On September 1, 1939, German forces rushed into Poland. To Adolf Hitler's surprise, the British and French kept their word. The two countries declared war on Germany. World War II was under way. It would last six years and kill over 60 million people.

Looking Ahead

The decade 1930–1939 was filled with hardship. People all over the world struggled to survive during the Great Depression. Things grew even darker with the start of World War II in September 1939. The war would dominate events of the next decade. It was the most destructive conflict in human history.

At first, the German and Japanese militaries won great victories. By early 1942, it seemed as though they could not be stopped. However, Americans fought bravely on many battlefields. They helped soldiers from Great Britain and the Soviet Union defeat the German army in Europe. They recaptured islands taken by the Japanese. The United States developed many new weapons. One was more terrible than the others: the atomic bomb. With a single blast, tens of thousands of people could be killed. Japan finally surrendered after two of its cities were destroyed by atomic bombs.

At the start of the 1940s, European countries controlled large overseas empires. But by the time World War II ended in 1945, Europe was left in ruins. The European empires began to break apart. People living in the British and French colonies in Africa, Asia, the Middle East, and South America began to seek independence. New countries were created all over the world.

Although the United States and the Soviet Union had worked together to defeat Germany, after the war ended the two countries became bitter rivals. A conflict known as the Cold War began in the late 1940s. The armed forces of the United States and the Soviet Union did not fight each other directly. Instead, the two superpowers tried to get other countries to support their political and economic systems, and to prevent the other side from gaining allies. The Cold War would continue until the early 1990s.

A Belgian mother and her children flee from fighting in Western Europe during the summer of 1940. World War II would be the largest and costliest conflict in history. By the time it ended in 1945, more than 60 million people were killed.

Chronology

1930—In March, President Herbert Hoover predicts that the nation's financial crisis will pass within sixty days. Instead, America sinks deeper into the Great Depression.

1931—In September, Japanese troops move into China's Manchuria region. It is the start of a long and bloody invasion.

1932—The Lindbergh baby is kidnapped in March. In May, the Bonus Army marches on Washington, D.C. Franklin D. Roosevelt is elected president in November.

1933—Roosevelt takes office in March. He begins his New Deal to fight the Depression. Adolf Hitler is appointed chancellor of Germany. In the United States, Prohibition is repealed in December.

1934—The outlaws Bonnie Parker and Clyde Barrow are killed by police in May. That same month, a vicious windstorm rakes the Dust Bowl.

1935—In August, Congress passes the Social Security Act. Italy defies the League of Nations and invades Ethiopia.

1936—In April, Bruno Hauptmann is executed for the kidnapping and murder of the Lindbergh baby. African-American track star Jesse Owens wins four gold medals at the Olympic Games in Berlin. President Roosevelt is elected for a second term.

1937—The German airship *Hindenburg* crashes in May at Lakehurst, New Jersey. Amelia Earhart disappears over the Pacific in July. Walt Disney's *Snow White and the Seven Dwarfs* is released. Full-scale warfare breaks out between Japan and China.

1938—At Munich, Britain and France give Germany the Sudetenland. In return, Hitler pledges no further aggression. Champion horse War Admiral is beaten by Seabiscuit in November.

1939—Hitler orders the invasion of Czechoslovakia in March. He signs a treaty with the Soviet Union in August. On September 1, the German army invades Poland. In response, Britain and France declare war on Germany. World War II begins.

Glossary

animator—An artist who creates moving cartoons.

chancellor—Title of the top government official in Germany.

dictator—A harsh and controlling ruler.

diplomat—A government official who deals with other nations.

drought—A long period without rain.

economy—The system of financial activity in a country or region.

improvise—To change, invent, or create without planning.

melody—The progression of single tones in a song; a tune.

natural resources—Objects from nature that are valuable to humans, such as wood, water, oil, and metals such as iron.

navigator—A person who plans the course of a ship or aircraft.

profit—Money earned from the sale of goods or services.

propaganda—Information used to sway public opinion; it is often false or misleading.

protester—A person who publicly opposes an event, law, or decision.

ransom—Payment demanded for the release of a person or object.

rhythm—The tempo or pace of a song.

treason—An act of betrayal against one's country.

Further Reading

Adams, Simon. *World War II*. New York: DK Publishing, Inc., 2007.

Bobek, Milan, ed. *Decades of the Twentieth Century: The 1930s*. Pittsburgh, Pa.: Eldorado Ink, 2006.

Campbell, Geoffrey A. *The Lindbergh Kidnapping*. Farmington Hills, Mich.: Lucent Books, 2003.

Degezelle, Terri. *Franklin D. Roosevelt and the Great Depression*. Chicago, Ill.: Heinemann Library, 2007

Feigenbaum, Aaron. *The Hindenburg Disaster*. New York: Bearport Publishing, 2007.

Haugen, Brenda. *Adolf Hitler: Dictator of Nazi Germany*. Mankato, Minn.: Compass Point Books, 2006.

Levey, Richard H. *Dust Bowl!: The 1930s Black Blizzards*. New York: Bearport Publishing, 2005.

Nardo, Don. *The Great Depression*. Farmington Hills, Mich.: Lucent Books, 2007.

Stone, Tanya. *Amelia Earhart*. New York: DK Publishing, 2007.

Venezia, Mike. *Franklin D. Roosevelt: 32nd President 1933–1945*. New York: Children's Press, 2007.

Internet Resources

<http://www.whitehouse.gov/kids/presidents/franklindroosevelt.html>
Read some fascinating facts about Franklin D. Roosevelt. The White House offers this profile of the former president.

<http://www.fbi.gov/libref/historic/famcases/lindber/lindbernew.htm>
Read an FBI report on the famous Lindbergh kidnapping case. It includes photos of the ransom notes and other evidence.

<http://www.ushmm.org/wlc/article.php?ModuleId=10005070>
This page explores the German invasion of Poland in 1939. It contains maps, photographs, and stories from people who were there.

INDEX

Picture Credits

Illustration credits: AP/Wide World Photos: 1 (bottom), 14 (bottom), 15, 19 (bottom), 34, 35 (bottom), 41 (bottom), 43 (bottom), 48, 51; courtesy of the Federal Bureau of Investigation: 28; Getty Images: 9, 11, 13 (bottom), 14 (top), 17, 21 (top), 41 (top), 45, 54; Michael Ochs Archives/Getty Images: 20; Time & Life Pictures/Getty Images: 24, 27, 52; The Granger Collection, New York: 18, 26 (top), 44; Selznick/MGM/The Kobal Collection: 46 (top); United Artists/ The Kobal Collection: 46 (bottom); Library of Congress: 1 (top left and right), 6, 7, 8, 10, 12, 13 (top), 16, 21 (bottom), 22, 31, 32, 33 (top), 35 (top), 38, 40, 42, 49; National Archives and Records Administration: 23, 26 (bottom), 50, 53, 55, 57; National Oceanic and Atmospheric Administration, National Weather Service Collection: 30; MGM/Photofest: 47; Warner Bros./Photofest: 29; courtesy of the Franklin D. Roosevelt Library: 4, 5, 33 (bottom); used under license from Shutterstock, Inc.: 19 (top), 25, 39, 43 (top); UN Photo: 36, 37.

Cover photos: AP Wide World Photos (*Hindenburg* crash); Library of Congress (migrant mother, Jesse Owens).